LATE NIGHT DRIVES TO YOU

Ry Reed

LATE NIGHT DRIVES TO YOU

Ry Reed

2

Thank you so much for purchasing this book! Don't forget to leave a review. I want you to share your thoughts with the world.

Thank you!

Books by Ry Reed

Poetry

PINK GRAPEFRUIT

WHITE ORCHIDS

GREY STORM CLOUDS

THE LITTLE RED POETRY BOOK CALLED
HEARTBREAK

WALKING ON THE MOON

A WELL OF THOUGHTS

LATE NIGHT DRIVES TO YOU

This is not a romantic tale. It's a tragedy.

I wasn't raised with positive representations of marriage and relationships. I knew plenty of married folks. My parents were married. My mother's friends were married. All the adults I knew at church were married, but the facade presented was not a fairy tale. It was a nightmare. Love. Love should be soft, meek, kind, polite, and not discrete. Love is patience. Love is sacrificial. Love is giving. Love is selfless. Love can withstand. Love is virtuous. Love is righteous and noble and generous. Taught and witnessing aren't the same. I can tell you how to love, but my actions show you the undeniable truth. You can't talk your way around your actions. What you do and how you act is plain and simple and telling.

I couldn't catch a break from my teenage years to young adulthood—heartbreak after heartbreak. I couldn't comprehend why I continued attracting the same person and energy. Why they left me all the same? Why couldn't they fill this hole within me? I had an epiphany. My eyes opened, and I could see. I was the problem.

I was a talented people pleaser—a well-known smuck. I was an enabler. Trained to put my emotions and thoughts on the back burner. I was a pushover, passive, modest, altruistic hero. I've had this savior mentality since childhood—the sacrificial lamb. To save everyone, I had to suffer and die slowly. I had opinions, but your views and well-being were prioritized far above me, and I was here to ensure your happiness. This ethos translated horribly into my relationships. I thought I was being a kind lover. My kindness and inability to voice my qualms made me a victim. I did suffer, rightfully so. I was stepped on and conditioned myself to stay quiet, though internally, I was detonating.

These poems and quotes are a cautionary tale. I advise anyone to learn from my mistakes and view relationships as testing grounds. First, heal from your past and confidently develop high self-esteem. Thicken your skin and only allow what you want. That's vital. Remember, you are worthy of love and are a prize, and a prize does not convince anyone to buy it. You're valuable whether they see your worth or not. Lastly, use your voice when the occasion arises. The second you feel offended, address your concerns. Do so the second you feel slighted. I ran from confrontation all my life when I should have bucked back. You have a voice for a reason. You have emotions as well. Don't ignore your feelings. Don't shy from discomfort. Don't fear losing someone for being honest. Your truth is yours, and the best you can do is live in a world where you respect yourself.

There were too many fragmented pieces to love, and I blamed you for not loving the mess.

CONTENTS

SPEED LIMIT 25

Was it when you said hello

Awkwardly shook my hand?

Was it when you hugged me?

Are you seeking warmth from my hands?

Was it after you laughed?

Because I wasn't as cool as I seemed

Was it when you first saw me?

In your dream?

Was it when I made sure you were okay?

You didn't feel good that day.

Was it when you told me you cared?

And I shared my intentions?

Act i

Happiness doesn't cost you a thing. Smiling is free. A good handshake should cost you everything, but it doesn't. Hugs are contagious mysteries. Laughter sticks to ribs. A friendly hello melts snow. "I miss you," cheeks glow.

I can't love you how you deserve to be loved until I learn to love myself.

A powerful message

Thunder loves storms

Like how a busy bee finds the sweetest flower

To ask for golden honey

A smooth stone follows a flowing river

To smooth its skin

A butterfly waits for its friend the wind

Clouds love a clear blue sky

And I love it when you say hi

We all love that one thing

The longer you stare

The more beautiful I become

Features brought to life

Incurred by time

You find beauty in the sculpture you revere

Art

If you laugh any harder

You'll forget to breathe

One more joke

One more

Please

Laughing

I wonder what sort of books you love to read?

I wonder if you like picnics

Or lying on the beach?

I wonder if you like scary movies

Or romantic comedies?

I wonder if you like cake

Or ice cream?

I wonder if you like hugs

Or kissing endlessly?

Is it blue or red?

Sky or boats?

Do you want an adventure?

Or to cuddle on the couch with me at home?

I wonder

It's unexplainable

What I feel for you

Where did you come from

I don't have the slightest clue

A gift to me

Two stars crossing paths simultaneously

You stare so dangerously

Why can't I think

Why can't I move

What was life before

I made your acquaintance

This late Friday afternoon

Sit by me

Skin turns maroon

Where oh where

You walk so close to the fire

I think you want to get burned.

Third degree

What could this be

Growing inside of me

Dwelling

Living

Breathing

An explosion of micro feelings

Have me low key

Acting funny

The source of my confusion

Soul moving

Wrapped around too tight

I see delusions

Of me and you

One plus two

Too many numbers

Subtract me

Minus you

Fifth grade

I go where my heart leads me…

Always to you

A drop of you

I drown in a sea of bliss.

Just a drop

You knew I was yours before I knew I belonged to you.

And once I knew you were mine,

You had me

Mine

This art cannot be duplicated

I admire it that much more

Memorizing every line before the picture changes

Mental shot

Your eyes invite chaos

This glittering essence within you

Knows all the right words to bait me

I hear through a closed mouth

A glimpse of mayhem

I can't resist

I'm a drunkard

High on oxytocin

I down you

Cup after cup

Stumbling on my way out

Before the bar closes

Drinking late

I'll keep you warm in the cold

Midterms

Were it simply us two

And

Time stilled

I'd have us sleep underneath the moon

Flurry dreams

Clouds of cream

Pillows made of honeydew

Our imagination is fatally flawed

Hallucinations

Maybe I should wake

And leave soon

Silly conversations

You dove, and I dipped my feet

The stakes were high

All bets are in

She wants fun, comfort, excitement, commitment, trust, passion, and all your attention.

Girls want

You talked

While I busied worshiping your existence

It wasn't what you said

The way you spoke

Words ripped apart

Syllables

Notes

Foreign languages

Dangled godly images

Threaded into my conscious

I hate to interrupt

Can you repeat what you last said

I'm listening

Tell me how beautiful your world is

Then paint it for me

Colors

When she's safe, she's miraculously vulnerable.

Safety net

I see as much as you show me…

Looking glass

It was more than chemistry that bonded us together

Fate

We laugh more than we talk

Perfect Chemistry

I stare for reasons…

Open availability

I dove in too quickly without checking the temperature…

Nervously licking your lips. You can't stop combing your hair. Body curving closer and closer. Hand hangs between you and me. Hanging onto my every word. There's an art to seduction, and a trained eye can spot your interest.

Seduction

Confidence is so attractive. The ability not to care about other people's opinions will draw fireflies to you.

Outdoor lights

She read you before you said a single word to her.

Side eyes

She likes a challenge, whether she realizes this about herself or not. The more unpredictable you are, kept on her toes, the more her interest grows. She'll wonder about you, rethinking all the minutes you spent with her. With the little bread crumbs you dropped, her appetite will be voracious.

Women

Teach me something new, and I'll admire you

Teach me

Brown eyes are dangerous because they're too warm and friendly.

Your eyes

I hope thinking of me keeps you awake all night…

In bed

Drunk on thoughts of me, impatiently waiting for
your next shot.

Day drinker

Talk to me

I have nowhere to go

Here is where I ought to be

Listening to you talk so freely

It's charming

Talk to me

Play with me

Until our backs hunch

And we fall laughing to our knees

Have fun

Some people you instantly fall in love with…

Talking about you

When she feels heard

She feels seen

She'll want to tell you more about her day

See me

Smiling

You might kill me

Eyes glazed over

Lost

Plotting how

You can get closer

Tables are horrible barriers

Table eight

My soulmate patiently waits for me to make a move.

I'm coming

The toughest exteriors

I swear have the softest insides

They're afraid to let you see

You're a softy

Your brown eyes conceal so many stories I wish to know

Eyes tale

Before I can love you

I need to work on me

Undo the programming of my past

Shed these layers of distrust

Become humble

Secure

Sure

Mentally, physically, and spiritually strong

So when you lean on me

I can support all your weight

Support system

There's nothing wrong with your nose, the slant in your eyes, your thick eyebrows, and your wide hips that stick together. You're not so flat stomach, your strong hands and round face. You look like a woman—a woman with features that accentuate your natural beauty.

Natural beauty

I can't wait to meet you all over again in my
dreams...

Sleep tight

I am in search of you

A quest

This map bears an X

There you are

My diamond

My pearls

My jade

My opal

My ivory

My world

I scavenge the sea

I plunder villages

I loot

I steal

Where are you

Where might you be?

Where are you

SPEED LIMIT 35

I closed my eyes so I could dream of you, and I

You and I

Relationships aren't equal. Half and half, that's not it. Being in a relationship doesn't ensure you'll do the same amount of work. Sometimes, you'll carry the brunt of the labor. Sometimes, their load will be heavier than yours. The workload fluctuates. That's why it's crucial to have a strong relationship. You never know what season you will be in life and when you aren't strong enough to lift your weight. When you're weak, they can hold you until you can stand again, and vice versa.

Why don't you come over here

And dance with me

I'll play your favorite song

Romance me

I'll follow you

Tell me when to go

Hands pressed on chest

Point your toes

Sweep me off my feet

I want to float

Carry me

Would you hold me?

We have all night

Our first dance

There isn't enough paint in this world

To capture you.

It's impossible to replicate

Your evolving hues

Portrait

Running through my mind

I chase you deeper and deeper into my heart

The chase

I came to say hello

My heart racing

Your presence is a remote control

This hold you have on me

Chains tighten

I paid the toll

The ferryman offers you my soul

Yours to forever own

Remote

Every far corner of my mind

Belongs to you.

Wherever I look

I find you

Waiting for me

Far corner

Holding your hand…

I learned how to stop time

Accidental magic

You don't make me smile

Much worse

You make me laugh

You make me laugh

We can talk about nothing and

I'll find our conversation

Interesting.

Convos

You're the missing piece of my heart I can't replace.
Without you, there's a dark space. I've tried to
substitute with all types of things. Nothing else can
complete this portrait of you loving me.

A sappy love song

My love language is you baring your soul

Let me see

Could it be that time stopped

Or

That my heart beat

Dimmed lights

Darkened rooms

Waiter

Drinks for two

Piano sets the mood

Quiet conversations

Stir temptation

I revel in how far apart you can be

To be so near

Intimate dinners

You can give me your heart.

I promise I won't drop it.

In safe hands

I'm learning to say "I love you" in a way you understand…

Lost in translation

You fell in love because I learned how to open you up…

Patient lover

It's easy to fall in love in the dark…

Tonight

Dialogue can flow in peaceful silence…

Look into my eyes

What does your love sound like?

A heart

A beat

And skip

Wedged below your fondness for me

A note sung low

You raise my tempo

Heart song

Hold me close

Legs tangle

Arms in knots

Hands glue together

Souls intertwine

You're nervous

So am I.

Time is all it took for us to find peace

Slumber

You snore?

Murmuring mi amor

Go to sleep

You inspire me to cast spells

and levitate objects with my mind

Inspiration

Your cheeks were made for soft kisses

__Cheekbones__

I appreciate the little things

Like how your hands

Curl inside mine

Little things

When you miss me

Tell me

Open dialogue

I am learning to trust you because you're so patient and loving.

Open door

You looked at me, and I set this city on fire.

The look

Without light

Fingertips paint you in darkness

A keen eye dots twinkling stars

Rounded moons

A touch of Mars

Forgotten under you and I

I'd never seen a galaxy so close

Painting in the dark

I would never waste a kiss…

Making a move

Cold but not freezing

Needing body heat

Was an excuse

I used to get closer to you

__January__

I'm glad you can't see my heart racing…

So close to you

I ask questions because I want to learn how your mind works

I listen because your words captivate my world

Hours upon hours

There are so many stories I wait to hear

On the edge of my seat

I wait impatiently for you to conclude

A thrilling tale

As your voice drifts to sleep

Nightly calls

I love it when your heart beats quicker because of me.

Heart pacer

It's easy to compare you to a star

I admire you both from afar

Admirer

Don't be shy

I cuddle as great as you think

Holds close

.

Do you see me falling, too?

I'm the darkest shade of rouge

I think I'm stronger

Then these brief hellos

Perpetually in a good mood

Do you think of me

As much as I think of you?

Could this be my time

I lied

I'm far from fine

It's impossible to be this far

Standing from behind you

Darker shade of rouge

Remembering the taste of powdered sugar on your
lips at 7:45 p.m.

Bakery

Take my hand

I'll fly you to the moon

Take my hand

I'll take my time learning your love languages first

How this machine works

It's the most important thing

Reading the manual first

Manual

I missed you today

Love letters

Tired of sneaking looks

I stare

Inviting you to want me

Dinner table

Your departure came as a shock

I was beginning to trust you

We hadn't reached the good part yet

Your love interest introduced themself

The plot unfolding

My scene ending

Fin

You taught me how to run barefoot on sand

Destination

Everywhere

The ocean is merely a playground, and we're here

To see everywhere and anything

Past the shoreline

In the deep

I drowned my first time with you

Drowned

I think of you when it rains

My mind plays

A story where it's you and I

Hugged close

Air cool

Pitter-patter sounds of droplets

Easing us to embrace

Raindrops

When they want you, they will be a quick, intentional dater. They won't play games. They'll want you and lay everything on a table for you to see. They won't be indecisive. When you say yes, they're ready to make you the center of their universe.

I don't want you to be with me.

I want you to grow with me.

Watering us

I search for your hand when I need you…

Need you

Play with me

Till our backs break

And we fall laughing to our knees

Run with me

Let's chase roses and butterflies in spring

Fight me

Battle my wits

I won't quit

Tickles are the antidote

Hike mountains and snow

Out of breath

Prank calls on payphones

Have fun

You act like yourself

When you're with me

Just me

I loved how much you talked about us too…

Secret Obsession

Craving my touch, it's harder for you to focus…

My touch

We stare into each other's eyes, admiring the cosmos.

Cosmologist

With you

I feel all the love

In this world

I had been missing

With you

If support is all you need

I have plenty

Your biggest supporter

Good eye contact. Watch how she unfurls her ribs.
Lean in, an inch or two. Be a kind ear. Tease her with
your eyes. Study her language. She'll say yes or no
with her hands and feet and smile.

Body signals

I studied you like art

A breathless sigh

Hallow cheekbones

A twitching nose

Parted full lips

Even Michelangelo

Would have been inspired

To create

Sculpted eyes

I found what I was missing in this world

And that's you

I found you

Occupy every corner of my mind, why don't you…

Go for it

The moon to my light

I worship the sand where your feet press

You walk with grace and pose

Strong back I can lean on

To my cheekbone

Tell me you love me so

Tell me

A kiss that made you forget where you were at.

I was worth the wait…

First kiss

Your stare

Is wicked, my love

Your thoughts are loud

How easily I can read them

I'm a student of you

I study the timidness my presence causes you

Squamish mannerisms

You hide so unsuccessfully

I play along

My gaze intent on you

I do not shy

When our eyes

Lock

Pretending to be unaware

Is so hard to do

Isn't it?

Dinner party

Falling in love with a kind, gentle being comes too easy.

There's no animosity

Only an available heart

Doors are open

Just for you

They are welcoming

So swiftly

Yanking your hand

Can you walk any quicker?

Kind-hearted

If you hug me

Promise to stay

One more hour

I kiss your cheeks because you're so sweet.

Sweet cheeks

Your flaws are what I find the most beautiful

Your flaws

A tug beneath my skin

Shakes frost off this

Below zero heart.

I see time threaded so tight

This cold heart

Warms back to life

Tied to you

Knotted around me

My soul is yours

Until you snip the string

Knotted

I stare at the things I want…

You

Let my voice be the last you hear and the first you talk to

Let me

Daydreaming of you

I won't get any work done.

Can't focus

I don't take small bites

I devour everything I want

Till there's nothing left

Except for scattered apparitions of

Who you were before

I consumed you

Bite

I make you feel understood

Because I take my time understanding you

Rather than complaining about you

You get me

Sitting beneath a star

I yearn to clasp you in my hands

And hold you

Where only I can

Marvel your dazzling light

Starlight

When you're tired, come rest with me

I will keep all your stubborn demons away

Bed rest

SPEED
LIMIT
65

You're a good reason to fight for.

I'm not going anywhere

Whenever I cross your mind, remember I'm yours,
and you're mine. A phone call away, messenger bird,
snail mail, smoke signal, spell out how much you
miss me in the clouds. I'm never too far from you.
I'm your heart.

I beat inside you.

Never too far

All the lovely swirls you drew on my skin…

Nails

Enchanted by the first stroke of you

Delicate

Fire kissed stone

A hardened heart forged to life

On a cold afternoon

First kiss

I'll build you a house

A home you can come undone

Remove stitched garments

Cotton socks

Let your hair down

There aren't any monsters or traps

I want you to take care

Be well

Relax in pleasant harmony

Sing a melody

On cool sheets

Our mansion in Belair

Come home

There's not much to say when you're in love

Except

I love you…

I do

I will…

Adore you.

Protect you.

Stay by your side.

Challenge and encourage you.

Make you laugh.

Kiss and hug you.

I'll die with your name on my heart and lips…

What else could you possibly be searching for other than me…

Tempting passionate stares

I take those as challenges

Don't charm the charmer

Not slick enough

I promise

You'll get bit

Saphire moons

Glorious shades of the brightest blues

Brown burned sea moss ember green

Rubies and pearls

Black devilish curls

Watered satin red velvet at your feet

Horizon peeks in caramelized pink

Yellow gold drips on heated flesh

Sun-loved skin toast genes

Heartbeats and lazy sounds

Greyish mountains blurred

In a white fog, we sleep

Rosy cheeks

When gentle fingers speak

Morning blanket

I've sipped wine

I've tasted you

And I can't tell the difference

You're both intoxicating

Wine tasting

I've planted you in my heart. A flower bloomed.
Mindful of you, I talk to you daily. How beautifully
you grow. A rose, thicket of thorns, tangle my heart
with your roots.

They made you from scratch

An unknown recipe

Never existed

Can't be replicated

Impossible to duplicate

Flavor so sweet

My teeth sink deep

Could this be the most decadent cream?

Baked to perfection

Angel food cake

Chilled strawberry cheesecake

Eclair

Is there extra to spare?

A mouthful more

Savory

Lingers on my tongue

Original recipe

Could there be anything savorer than my teeth sinking
into your skin…

Bloodlust

Would you stay another minute?

I need one more with you.

Would you hold me for another hour?

I'll make it quick.

Will you love me for another day?

That's it.

Then you can leave.

Stay with me for eternity?

You can go afterward.

One more minute

Restless nights

I wrestle with my thoughts

Because you consume my dreams.

It's the same dream

Dreaming of you and me

In a world where it's you and I

We close our eyes

Bodies lost in unconscious reality

Dreaming dreams

If I could slow down time and hold this

Moment in my hands forever

I would

Pause button

I loved you more in the dark

Ebony skin

To be close:

When I feel alone, your name comes to my mind.
Who else would I call? You. The first I go to when I
need help. The first I call when I'm sad. An
unmeasurable, priceless love. Coveted. I don't take
your attention for granted. Give and take. We share
almost everything. Time strengthens our bond.
Memories immortalize us. Here, for a good laugh, cry,
or vent. We grow through multiple seasons.

What is trust?

I trust you won't break my heart when I give it to you.

It's hard for me to put all my faith in you, but you've shown how dependable you are. I believe in us. I'm afraid but I will follow you anywhere.

Dip her into your coffee

And she'll make it sweet

A cup of sugar

I work hard

Long days

In anticipation

Of seeing you

All night

Soon my love

You flirt with your eyes

Frowns I despise

Grins are all mine

Fine lines

Laugh lines

I'll write my name on the dotted line

You are my reason

The season

Time flies by

With you by my side

I stare at the ceiling.

Thinking

Of only you.

Memories play on rewind

Of you

Only the strongest can stand with you during a storm.

Talking to the wrong person will leave you feeling empty and unheard.

Ask yourself this: when you needed them the most, where were they? Did they appear or disappear?

Come over here

My arms are waiting…

Hurry up

I make thinking of you a daily habit

I pencil you in

In my mind

It's hard not overindulging

My calendar is booked

On my mind

Your lips share so many secrets

I can't confess to another soul

You've hinted at a desire

I taste freedom

I listen carefully

Careful not to miss a word

Passionfruit

What matters most is how I made you feel.

It matters

Is that you?

In the abyss of this nowhere

I've visited lately.

A distilled image I can't contain

You've set this rickety heart ablaze

Only where it truly matters

Lost in dark matter

I'll make it last

Protected in unbreakable glass

We'll last longer

I'll count the hours

Trap you in a tower

Devour

Greedily hoarding too much power

Dark matter

We think we have all night to talk until we fall asleep.

Sleepyhead

Your body speaks languages only my soul can interpret

Comprehending long hugs

Heavy lidded gazes

Parted lips

Strolling through a maze

Searching for hands

Confessions in my ears

Between the rows of invitations

Yearning for a postcard in the mail

Break these chains

I pray they rust

I go where there's no sun

Body speaks

Soak me

To the last drop

Leave nothing good for waste

Bought ripe

And bitter

Unique

An acquired indulgence

You'll adore the longer you sip

The more you'll crave

Bottle after bottle

Days lost

Down me in doses

Take and cherish

This wine ages beautifully

Pour a glass

I don't mind burning for you…

Sounds romantic and dark

You have a venomous bite

As sharp as your teeth

I anticipate infliction

Snake charmer

At the stroke of three

I feel the stroke of your hand

It slowly dances on my back

Soft made pressure

My arms instinctively tighten themselves around your
chest

I haven't left

My arms confess

Fall back to sleep

Daylight warms our skin

I'm still here

A kiss

Maybe two

Or three

Endless

Fly as close to the sun as you please

My flames caress your feathers gracefully

I live to watch you soar

Fire is a deception

Death is galore

To the sun

Loving loving you…

The little things

Built a bridge

Your side

My side

Thicker than glue

The finest material

Nonetheless

My love

This foundation doesn't shake

Can withstand any earthquake

Hands joined

I will never let you go

Bridge

Stuck on me

How I planned it to be

You watch my roots spread feverishly

To the lake and ponds

River's flow

Quenching of thirst

The temptation of water

Bit your lips

Resisting urges, I've envisioned

Years ago.

Why don't you make yourself at home

And drink

Come back tomorrow

Cool water

You came and left too quickly for me to hold on…

Gone too soon

My hands search for you under the covers

How glad they are

To softly caress

Your smile

Your chin

Your nose

Searching for you

I feed your soul. That's why you love my company.

Soul food

Learning to love you will take time, and I'm a good student.

Your soul belongs to me

And only me

The appearance of freedom

I give you

Until the rope around your heart

Is tugged

I let you go

Only so far

You walk

But run home

When I call you

Belongs to me

We have so much chemistry

It's physically

Impossible to atomically

Divide our atoms

From supercharging

This is science

Tell me where you want to go, and I'll take you there.

Where to

Missing me miss you makes you miss me more…

Damn, I miss you

On nights like this,

I think about you

When the temperature drops

And I have you to keep me warm

Nights like this

I lay on your chest for hours, listening to the same
song

on repeat.

Repeat

Standing by your side means

Standing with you

Supporting you

Taking care of you

Caring your burden with you

Crying with you

Celebrating with you

Having faith in you

Trusting you

Relying on you

Taking your advice

Growing with you

Protecting you

Here I stand

I will support your ideas

Your successes are my successes

When you look good

I look even better

I go you

We fall asleep the same way we always do

In each other's arms

__Good night love__

I collected all your tears

Planted them in seas

I never lost count of all the times you cried

Over painful dreams

Made dreadful by powerful blows

That swept you off your toes

I cleaned each tear

Carried you home to a tower

I ran you a hot shower

Offered warm towels

To dry your face

Your tears

In me

There's all the love in the world

A love made for you

Molded from your heart

My love

Fits like a hand in a glove

Key in a lock

Honey in tea

Sweet dreams and a good night's sleep

My love

Is just for you

My love

My love

Questioning my love for you

A little or a lot

The keys to my heart

Open this door

Have a look

See for yourself

Keys to my heart

Stay with me

A moment longer

My life depends on how

Many hours we spend

Ravishing skin

With teeth and wicked grins

I pin you down

Slowing your departure

Stay with me

My tempest

You drive me wild

Devious little spirit

Plotting schemes

I plan my next heist

Your time

Is the bounty

Heist

You have my mind, body, and soul.

What do you want next?

All yours

The highest level of comfort:

Finding peace in silence. There's no need to fill the air with chatter. You know everything about everything going on in my life. You and I do a great job communicating. Long drives in the car, we can relax, listen to music, and nap while you hold my hand in your lap. I enjoy your silence. You find peace in mine. We can happily exist in our thoughts while in our company.

Two-hour drives

We don't have to discuss my day

All I want is to lie on your chest

A movie to watch

As you feed me your Starbucks

Is all I want to do

Long day

I spend most days getting to know you

You change and grow every day

You evolve

I call it daily happenings

Seasonally emerging

I need to catch up

Before I miss any

New developments

How are you today

Find all the peace you're looking for in my arms.

Peaceful soul

Ask her why after every question to delve further into the conversation. Squeeze as much information out of her as possible. She has so much to share. Then, ask her how it made her feel. Then she'll tell you what really happened after that.

Tea time

Painting lips with a stroke of my fingertip

This art

Does not stay still

Painting

I can't force you to tell me how you feel. I'll ask once, twice, maybe three times, but the decision to vent falls on you. My door is open. You can enter whenever you like. I believe in open communication but I can't be there for you unless you let me in. I don't know the problem until you bring it to the table. Walking away, ignoring my phone calls and texts, and pretending you're fine separates you further from me. Let your guard down, and be honest. I'm not perfect. I make mistakes. I'm willing to listen.

You don't have to accept anything that infringes on your values and morals. You have two decisions. Leave or stay. Remember that when you stay. You're reinforcing their behavior. Not expressing your disdain perpetuates your mistreatment. Not confronting them removes your power.

Pride gets in the way of seeing your mistakes because you think you're right. This doctrine leads to losing everything. Pride is living with tinted glasses. You only see and feel what you do. Your ego is failing you. You'll be intolerable to be around and defend.

They'll chase you once they realize how much they
need you…

I miss you

You're too stubborn to walk back to me…

So stubborn

When my expectations fell short of reality

I refused to believe it was an illusion

Hard to see

A cup of you is all I need

An ounce

A drop

Will help me breathe

Some for all the years you watched me bleed

Selfish for needing more

Obsessed I know

Imagining this love is wrong

Disappointment is a familiar home

Begging at my lowest of lows

For water on a lonely road

Just a drop

Your words tell me maybe so

Maybe no

I thought we were close

People in the background vanished

Ghosts.

Clear as day

You say what must be said

Buried

Confirmed dead

My heart in my head

Tension thick enough to be seen

Why are you so mean

Green

I go the opposite way

You refuse to let me go

I stay in the cold

Stay

I asked the moon

To sing a song

And he sang

The blues

Blue moon

You learned how to hurt me in every language…

The language of love

I knew you, and that scared you.

Scared of vulnerability

Do you want to see me?

You miss me?

You were on my mind all day

Stop playing around.

You can't go another day?

Do you want me to drive up?

Yeah

Okay

Give me an hour

I'll call you when I'm outside

How it starts

I stepped on dried roses and thorns to hold you

Soles bloody

I kissed you hard enough

You never looked down

Bloody roses

I don't expect you to keep your door open forever. If they don't want to come inside, shut it.

So angry

You ignored this gaze from across this desolate room

I can sense how pissed off you are at me

My fault for not thinking my schemes through

Mad for not trusting you

I irritated a salty wound

Your heart

Your faith in me

Staring at you while you talked to everyone in heaven but me

Was punishment enough

Closed the gates

I couldn't locate the keys

Unwanted guest

There's wisdom in silence and listening.

I made myself too available in hopes of catching some of your feelings.

Fishing

Hurting

You'll question everything they've done to you.

I need space

You have a voice, and you should use it.

Stand up for yourself

If you wanted to see me, you would be at my door.
Excuses are bullshit. Effort goes a long way.

When you miss me, honey

Give me a visit

I know I'm hard to quit

Yes

Kiss me

Hug me, honey,

I'm a little dangerous

Teeth

Fangs

My eyes hypnotize

When you miss me, give me a visit

I know I'm hard to quit

Yes

Cottage in the woods

It's hard to walk away

My pace starts to change

When you decide to look my way

Navel cracks

Molts into a bruised state

The truth is so hard

You've been gone too long

This distance feels like miles

Your stories are all lies

I can't backpack back because of memories

This space you've made are walls to me

But I hear your voice in my dreams

I have to leave now

I'll be in the next town running to you because I never
had anybody

I'll hold you like I am that one somebody

But I'm strong enough

To know when enough is enough

Enough is enough

Where did you go?

Twinkling nights

Bed so cold

I've walked from hell and back

Pleading you say my name

Through this disconnected phone

Tell me

Where did you go?

Disconnected

Taken but not stolen

Missing but present

Yours but mine

Beats for one

Alive for me

Here and gone

To exist for one

Here for none

Except you

Conditional love is madness

I help you reload a gun

To use when I'm no longer fun

Taken

I stood where you told me

I haven't complained

I wanted to, but I knew the rules

You explained them frequently

I didn't envision spending my time

Waiting for you to save me

From imprisonment

But the rules are the rules

And I agreed to spend a season with you

The rules

I don't know what's wrong with you until you tell me. I get it. You're not used to opening up and showing anyone every side of you. But you have to. We'll never move forward until you get it off your chest. And if they love you, really love you, whatever you tell them won't scare them. They should be able to listen to you while you're vulnerable.

You're too attached to who you want them to be.
You're not hurt. You're disappointed.

Damn, I need to sit

You try to hide all the pain they've inflicted on you…

Dying inside

I was polite when I should have been direct and told you how much I missed you…

I really missed you

How badly you wanted me to stay eats me up every day. I should have canceled my plans and made you my only plan.

Reschedule

Mad at you

I stayed away for as long as I could

It was torture

The daily reminders

Intoxicating memories

Lustful thoughts

Your sweet laughter

My little joy

I called you right back

Called you

At a distance is precisely where you want me

Too close is bothersome

Further out is just right

Personal makes you squirm

A mysterious silhouette is easier to paint

Missed phone calls are per usual

Chasing you is expected of me

Over a fence

I stop at a gate

How long do you want me to stand in your picture

Move three steps to the left

I'm out of frame

Couple's portrait

Love her wrong, and she'll grow cricketed.

Bent flower

Pushed me away

Found out

How much you cared

Too proud to admit it

Rather daydream than fix it

What was

Before disappearing

On Monday

Could have been

I can't fight for someone who constantly lets me go.

Empty-handed

Break her trust too often, and she'll never trust you again. If she says she does trust you, she's lying. She's waiting for you to pull another stunt.

Stunt man

Your opinions mattered more than mine. I placed your needs before what little needs I had. I followed your lead, and you needed to figure out where you were going. I catered to your problems, believing they were my problems. Unbalanced, I should have measured our relationship equally.

Equals

I see nothing wrong with putting your foot down and giving ultimatums. It's either you or their bad habits, and they can't have both.

Pick one

When you have no one to talk to

You tend to lock so many emotions inside

They don't bury well

And fester in your chest

Waiting for impact

Not an outburst

Or out-of-character rage

It's overwhelming feelings

They have nowhere to go but out

Tantrums are exhausting

As exhausting as it was hiding

From everyone

Including yourself

Lost it all

Your unhappiness is not my responsibility.

I can't change the color of the sky

The direction of a breeze

The shape of a tree

The sting from a bee

The hum of a hummingbird.

I cannot make you happy

If all you are is unhappy

You took that shape

And all you are is misery

Not my responsibility

Forgiving you so quickly, my self-esteem was in shambles.

Looted

You should feel wanted and needed

Because I want and need you

Wants and needs

Tired of loving you with this broken heart

It's not enough

I don't have much to give

And what little I do have

I hid

I played a hesitant game

I lost because I gave less than you did

Broken toys

You will be lonely was the last flavor I tasted drinking
you.

Expiration date

Once

Twice

Three times

This wasn't fun

Playing with my insecurities

Got me in my feelings

I feel lonely

I blamed it on you

For believing love had levels

Your devils persuaded you

They told you I wasn't fun

You did not run

Stayed

To hurt me

You cared none

I was a chump

Chump

I built you up

But the final results weren't for me

I thought it was mine

That's why I did the hard work

And cleaned

All your windows were broken before me

I put a door where there was none

I guarded you

Picket fence

You asked me to paint it the same color as the sun

I look back dumbly

At locked doors

Stolen keys

A welcome mat

Not to clean my feet

The "I can't talk to you right now" f**ked me over…

That's fine

When I sense you coming

You're going

And when I leave

You want me back

Coming and going

I'm taking over the world, so you'll notice me…

World domination

It was so hard trusting you after you obliterated my trust.

Destroyed

I failed to see how hurting you hurt me. How staying angry at you made you withhold your light from me. How not being honest made you feel untrustworthy. How sheltering my thoughts made you block your thoughts from me. Losing enthusiasm made you feel unmotivated. How not considering you made you put yourself first. My lack of effort provoked you to look for attention elsewhere.

I apologize.

I apologize

You were too selfish, and I was too forgiving

It was a game we played

Where you hurt me

I forgave you

So you could hurt me again

Bad game

You have every right to feel angry if they made you
mad.

Madmen

I feel unimportant

There are better things to do

Better things to watch and see

I was here and there, and nowhere

Irrelevant as the words from my mouth

Had I been a statue

You would have appreciated

Art over your creation

Very irrelevant

We sat at the same table

Eating separately

Late dinner

I stand close

I hate to be far

This space you made between us

We're coexisting in two atmospheres

I want your hand

You reel back

My lips on your cheek

Your head turns

I stare into eyes that look through me

Not at me

Lost in matter

I don't know where you went

I scanned heaven for months

Without a hint or trace

Lost in space

Leaving her when she's fragile, she feels abandoned.

I'm leaving

True love is stronger than a petty argument.

Let's talk

People will disappoint you. Don't take everything to heart.

She's misunderstood because you're not listening to her.

Take notes

I can ask you to stay

But it's your choice to leave.

It's up to you

Without trust

You won't believe anything I say

Trust me

You can't open up if you're still internally bleeding.

Car Accident

Drain her ragged

Her responses will be as dry and brittle

As her moods

To the bone

She can snap at any minute

Dry as a bone

It's not what they say that's heartbreaking

It's what they do that has you lost for words

And emotions

Emotionless

True love lasts for an eternity

It doesn't stop when you're tired.

True love

You contemplated leaving me long before I was aware

And I swore to fight for you

After I became aware

Awareness

You don't know how sensitive you are

Until someone close to you hurts you

And you implode

So angry

One phone call away

One drive

One second from saying the hell with this

You've proved your point

Taught me a lesson I'll never forget

Let's mend this gap between us

Meet me in Amsterdam

You've proved your point

Rejected

Hard for me to feel close to you

Insecurities and receding

Is how I cooped.

Told not today

I can't

I have other things to do

It reaffirmed the little person in me

Of how unwanted I was

Better to mind my business

Blocking how bad rejection felt

Not today

She questions your love

Because you've made her think

You don't find her beautiful anymore

She'll say this

"You don't like me."

Pull over the car

And show her how wrong she is

Don't tell her

She won't believe you

SHOW her

She has to see your need for her

Hot on your lips

To soothe this doubt plaguing her mind

Show me

You weren't alone, missing us. Gemini made brightest at night, your voice a beacon of hope, and I was your hail mary to carry you to the next morning. We loved talking ear to ear. The ramblings of divine souls finally made contact, lost in space. We found one another floating on planes, boarding the same train. You exited early. I stayed on for too long waiting for you. The kisses I blew were for you drifting in space.

Space travel

Ignoring how bad you feel only makes you feel worse

Worse

I wander in search of the feelings you once gave me…

Where oh where

She'll think you no longer want her if she goes too long without hearing your adoration.

Of course I want you

Loving you is loving myself

Harming you cut my wrists

Abandoning you

I deserted my home

Ignoring you

I stopped looking at my reflection

Yelling at you

My ears ring

You are me

I am you

You are my mirror

I stare at

Man in the mirror

Cheating isn't what killed me

How well you facilitated the lie

That laid me to rest

Died peacefully

Alone,

I bled to death

In despair

Sorting through old memories of you

I fabricated in my head

The heart monitor flatlined

Scrolling to the past

I uttered your name

Gasping my final breath

Your absence

Stabbing me

The scene ended

The audience cheered

I was not an actor

The final act

I knew you were fire and touched anyway.

Fire danger

Loving you destroyed me

And I loved how much of a wreck I was

Recklessly in love

It killed me to let go

That's why I held on to the very end.

Hold my hand

So in love

You were my drug

I pierced into my veins

Anticipating

A rush

I wanted to live

High

My appetite met

Still unsatisfied

I dropped you off

Preparing for my next fix

Next fix

I'm everything you need, and that terrifies you…

Good option

Insecure because the last one

Set your heart on fire

You walk light

Burns from your past

Ache when touched

Trust is given

Eventually, I will get hurt

Crosses your mind

Far too often

You wear scars like a badge

You heartbreak solider

Burn survivor

Longing for you when the candles blow out…

Lights off

She might be having a bad day. That's why she has an attitude or a short fuse. There's not much you can do but remind her that you're here and ready to listen when she wants to talk about her day. She's human. She's not going to be perfect. Try your best to be understanding.

I understand

We fell in love so fast that we didn't know where we were going…

Full steam ahead

I was jealous. You knew that. I struggled watching you soak up all the attention in every room. I played it cool, cooler than the drink I couldn't stop drinking to cool my frustration.

Cool lemonade

Even if I said you were beautiful and meant it, you wouldn't believe me…

You're beautiful

Missed phone calls

More like ignored

I sensed the end but hung on

Bad reception

I craved you more than air.

I tried to live without air.

I died without you.

Oxygen

Hearts sink when they're lied to…

Rejection doesn't make you heartless.

Rejection toughens the walls around your ribs to protect them from future damage.

Thick skin

She notices when you stop trying to be the person she
fell in love with…

Minor details

I still keep my porch lights on for you.

The key is under the mat

Me loving you isn't enough to make you love yourself. I can't make you feel whole. I can't be the reason why you get out of bed. Only you can make yourself feel whole. You must be the reason for your happiness, the wind beneath your sails, and your inspiration once you find your source of happiness and joy. No one will be able to take that from you.

We were broken and tried to fall in love. Together, there weren't enough pieces to complete us.

We act tough because we hide how sensitive we are on the inside. Under all the leathers, masks, and layers, someone small lives yearning to be loved. To be hugged. To be heard. To feel safe and secure.

Cry when you need to. Holding it in, appearing all together and in control, is a bluff. You're human, and humans have emotions. Grief is an emotion. So is sadness. Your body is responding to triggers. Suffocating your feelings and pushing them down will accumulate over time. You're not invincible. Let it come. Let it flow. Process. Come to terms with feeling. Validate your feelings. Respect your feelings. Note why they came and how that makes you feel. Then and only then can you begin healing. Cry when it comes and reflect.

I've never seen you alone. You were alone once, and that fear threw you into the wrong arms. They were different but the same. They promised to love you but hurt you in the same fashion. They came charming, tall, handsome. They knew you were broken. They were broken, too. They preyed on your vulnerabilities and insecurities. It started fast and heavy, falsified destiny. They painted you a picture and drew you a life. It sounds nice. You give them what little love you have left, and they obliterate it. Phone calls came frequently, but now calls come too few. Promises are forgotten. It was toxic from the start. You didn't choose him using your head. You used your heart. Broken, castaway, your life is in disarray. Your children sort through all your pieces, frantically rearranging them into a body to love them after your heartbreak.

I'm learning how to accept my flaws. All eighty-two of them. I'm not perfect, but in progress. I'm hurt, but I'm healing. I'm busy unlearning everything taught to me. I'm a smidge selfish, robustly stubborn, a pinch sensitive. Emptying my cup, I'm starting fresh. I will make something good out of the bad. Something sweet out of the sour. Something soft out the hard.

I felt you slipping from my hands

Devastatingly

I squeezed tighter

Choking an unresponsive body

That sought death

Depending on the rise and fall

Of the gauge

I had no access to

Pulling

Begging

Pleading

The pulse would not return

Even on life support

I refused to accept reality

And pull the plug

Gone too soon

Out of touch

Not my mind or spirit

I count the days spent without us

As you do too.

Memories of you

Enough to pass the time

Walking without a clue

Of when I'll find a way back

To where we first met

Long before I left

Finding my way back

Heart beyond the soul

Cut me in two

Passion flows through this body

Pumping in my veins

Cut here

Saw there

Take all you need

Anything that beats

Use it to make yourself whole

Heart transplant

I thought I would die without you

It turns out I was wrong

Much worse happened…

Here lies me

Where did I go?

Somewhere

To the corners of your mind and beyond

To haunt you for all eternity.

All it takes is a thought

A reminder

Burning for my touch

A lonely night

I appear in whatever form you need

To see

Feel

Crave

The conversations we have are what

You create

What I do

I'm yours to take

Only here to stay

This night in May

In your memories

You say you're too hurt to look back

But when you think no one is watching

You do.

Amnesia

You must have forgotten what they did

To you

You leisurely walk back

To your preferred doom

Not true love

Just gloom

There are still good people in this world

Waiting to meet you

Soon

I once bore my soul.

There was no encore

I decided it was best to hide

Underneath layers of denial

Too heavy to peel

Last show

All you wanted was me.

You wanted me in your arms at night

To lay on my chest in the morning.

A French breakfast

Tea, baguette, strawberry jam

Avocado, toast and ham

Dreamy views of the Ivory Coast

Sailboats, wine, and a back to mold into

Never too far

Fingers in my hair

A kiss on the cheek

Needing to embrace

Back to bed

Back to my arms and love

A boring Monday

What you wanted

God made her with fire, so she never loses herself in darkness…

There's no buried treasure here.

Was found and taken and never

Replaced.

The worst pain I felt

Was missing you.

When I missed you

I understood how much I need you

And needing you

Made me regret neglecting you

My arrogance and pride
Stopped me from treating you better.

Too young

Flowers weep before they bloom…

To weep (cry) means to express sorrow by weeping. But what is sorrow? To feel deep distress caused by loss, disappointment, and misfortune. So, to weep means to cry, understanding loss. But to feel sorrow, you have to cry (liquid). Let's compare this to a flower in bloom—the seed. For a seed to become a flower, it has to endure the pain of growing. Seeds grow alone. They take root in the dirt, void of light, and in the cold. What helps a seed become a flower? Water. A seed needs moisture to grow. When you're at your breaking point and cry, you feel and understand your pain, disappointment, and loss and weep. Compared to a flower, you are also growing, feeling your pain so you can bloom.

I will construct the tallest building in the world

And stand on top

Where my pride can comfort me

From how small I used to be

Far below

Builder

You have to let them regain your trust after they fragment it. You're inviting them in too soon without fully digesting their actions.

You should never be cussed at. You should never be talked down to. They are responsible for their actions and words from morning to night, spring to winter, victory to loss. Their words are their responsibility. Words cut deeper than any weapon because words stick to you forever. You never forget being called ugly and by whom. You never forget how insensitive a teacher was to you. You never forget being called dumb or stupid. When you're old and grey, you'll remember all the hateful things people said to you. So, hold people accountable for what they say. Make sure they comprehend how badly they hurt you. And let them earn your trust back. Don't run back into their arms. Let them earn you because, for every action, there is a consequence.

Not responding is a response. It means no.

I gravitate towards good vibes, positive energy, wealth, and healthy relationships.

You're not boring…

You're at peace.

Chaos, yelling, hitting, cursing, acting out, throwing tantrums, stirring drama, cheating, lying, not communicating, deception, uncontrollable, emotionally immature, childish… That's not peaceful. People drawn to those demons don't desire a healthy, calm life.

Could I have been sweeter?

The sugar you add to your coffee?

How sweet

Would I be

Heating cold from your extremities

A wispy vapor

Soft on your mouth

Tender on your lips

A sweet vanilla caramel smell

Would you have drunk me?

Inhaled me?

Would I linger on your skin?

A savory thought

Would you order me again and again?

Add sugar

A guard protects your sensitive heart

Ransacked before me

You allowed too many in

And too many failed

You preserved

With iron and bolts

An impenetrable barrier was the price to be paid

To clot the bleeding

Too tall to see over

Too thick to break

Too wide to go around

Too deep to dig under

Patience was the last resort

And with that

The door merely cracked

Nothing more

Nothing less

Patient lover

It's hard breathing without you.

Lungs

There will always be a quiet place to rest on a mountaintop.

Thinking place

The lion playing with the sheep

The sheep playing the lion

My hand's thimble

You can approach without fear

No bite or bark

No razor-sharp teeth

Talons or claws

A gentle beast

I do not stand menacingly or tall

My attitude is controlled

Timid eyes saw blood far too soon

Taught to stalk

I walk with a puffed chest, but my roar is kind

Hello

Only predators can spot the beast

The meek underestimate the isolated, eerie sheep

Sheep's clothes

Heated memories cause you to stumble over how good it used to be

Heated moments

You can be with anyone, but not everyone can help you become a better version of yourself.

Wisdom teaches you to operate in love and to distance yourself from toxicity.

Having high self-esteem would have saved you from a lot of bullshit.

Hard lessons

I can't compete with the sun

Nor night

Sand is far more friendly

The ocean hugged you tighter than I ever could

The mountains gave you views I could never

Trees shade you longer

My arms couldn't bear the heat

The birds sang you songs you wanted to hear

The streets took you places I could never guide your
feet

Buildings were warmer than me

Blankets cuddle you longer

Clothes shape your skin perfectly

There was nothing left for me to do or be

I wasn't enough to meet your needs

Those jobs were taken by

Everything and everyone other than me

No job openings

Sensitivity is not a weakness.

It's your greatest strength.

Very sensitive

I try not to look back when I'm hurt…

Time to myself

You haunt me

Your name finds me in every phase of my life

A simple name

Magical

An indication that you won't leave me alone

Your smile is seen on similar souls

Grin more to the right than left

Quirky attitude

Defiant stubbornness

Your spirit roams

Flesh to flesh

Will you ever let me go?

Haunting spirit

Shoot where the vital organs are missing…

Heart

You can't give me your heart until you're healed.

Still hurts

You have a horrible habit of pushing me away when you're crying. I don't know how to love you when I can't find you…

You're bitter because you won't forgive me

Hanging onto the past is all you know

No one taught you how to accept

And let go

Bitter tinge

I learned to give the person I love time to process their feelings and not to rush them into deciding because I'm impatient. Hours, days, weeks, months, I have to respect their boundaries whether I like the results or not.

A good thing lasts a year.

A sure thing lasts an eternity.

A sure thing

It's easy shedding someone you don't care about…

Very easy

Good communication is everything. It's the difference between guessing how someone's feeling and knowing precisely what they need from you. Bad communicators leave you in the dark. They're hard to read. They're unstable and constantly flip-flopping their decisions at your expense. They neglect to tell you how they're feeling.

It's impossible to make an unhappy person happy. They were miserable before you got there. That's all you need to know.

Choose people who want you. Your life will be indefinitely easier if you think this way.

I forgave you because I was ready to move on…

Wait for people to come to you. If you've been good to them, they'll contact you. If they don't, they never appreciated what you offered. It's their loss. Not yours.

If you ever felt like I let you go

This portrait was painted wrong

I never let you go

I gave you room to grow

Stretch

Run

Where you jumped

I was below

My arms extended

Prepared to catch you if you fell

Let go

Feeling irritated, stay calm. There's no need to raise your voice. You don't have to slam a door. You don't have to throw a cup. Stay calm and collect yourself. Your voice is your greatest tool. With it, you can clarify your problems maturely. Children have tantrums. Adults talk.

Humans aren't perfect. We fall short. Placing high expectations on people ensures heartbreak. Be forgiving when they've earned your forgiveness.

I forgive you

All you can do is contact them and be available. Your job is done if they don't answer your calls or respond to your messages. No one will look back and say you didn't try. You did. The hard part is picking up your ego and brushing rejection off. I know how bad rejection feels, but you can't sit and dwell on it. Over a billion people live on this planet, and I'm positive a few would love to meet you. Stop texting and calling them and heal. Prospects are waiting for you. Get ready and be in a good mental place before they find you.

You didn't love me. You tolerated me.

Uncovering the truth

Those cracks on your heart can be repaired with love.

Heart repair

I thought you were real, but you were a ghost.

Ghosting

I talk to myself about you working through our issues.

Self-therapy

The lack of eye contact is noticeable.

Pretending I don't exist is worse

Or perhaps all the missed messages

Irritated me the most

How you thought I wouldn't notice

Baffles my soul

Break

A stone made of glass

This shell is soft to the touch

Softer than most

A durable exterior

Is the biggest plot twist

Stone exterior

Bottomless well

My arms paddle

There is no room

To swim

Only to stand still

And float

Standstill

It's hard loving when you refuse to address all the pain you've felt...

It's hard

You don't want to be liked. You want to be respected.
You'll rest easier that way.

If you have to walk away for them to realize how much you mean to them, keep walking. Don't turn around. Don't look back. Keep walking forward.

Day by day

I piece myself back together

One piece at a time

Day by day

They can't feel or understand you when they're disconnected. That's why you're frustrated. You're misunderstood. You're interacting with people who aren't connected to you. They're in proximity to you.

You never knew how badly you hurt me because I never told you. That's my fault, and I apologize to myself for not telling you the truth.

Staying with someone who is comfortable leaving you will damage your self-esteem.

Runaway bride

I saw you in the city

Did you miss me?

Was it difficult to walk past me?

Eyes slyly meet

Hard because you don't recognize a girl with a clean
face

Ripped and shredded

She repaired cracked sidewalks and worn streets

Drying concrete

Removed tagging's

She painted now open above a looted pet store
brimming with doves

Miles between us

Not this street

Street

Learning to trust people after surviving a toxic relationship will be hard.

Walking alone to talk to yourself is healthy.

Let's go for a walk

Selfish people do not apologize.

A fact

Before you can give love, you must love yourself. Love is both an inner and outward endeavor. To give love, you have so much love within you that you can pour your love physically, mentally, and spiritually into another person.

It will take years to rebuild yourself again…

In the works

If abandonment was my kryptonite

Then I died

Forreal

It's surreal

To see a knife in your hand

Cut slowly

Stick to the plan

Death crept leisurely

I shrieked

In shock

My lungs deflating

Justifying your assault

The knife penetrates

Stopping until I'm a regretful memory

Die slowly

Overlooked

Mistreated

Abused

Unseen

Forgotten

Misunderstood

If this is all you've been given

You'll believe this is all you deserve

You don't deserve this

Knowing your worth looks like letting them leave

And opening the door

When they want to go

I'll walk you out

I fought for you

And my prize was an empty container…

No prize

There's nothing left to break

It's all bits and pieces

Too little to salvage

Together like before

Bits and pieces

Wonderful dating advice:

Ask them out twice. That's it. On two separate occasions. Play it cool and ask them out. Don't pressure, bug, or guilt trip them. If they say no the first time, end the conversation with "That's fine. Let me know when you're free." If you don't hear any news from them after two weeks to a month, ask them out again. If their response is the same, "I have to check my schedule," "I'm swamped," "My family," or "I don't know," they aren't interested. This isn't a bad thing. They don't want to spend time with you or can't decide if you're a worthy investment. Reel in your energy and redirect it towards people jumping over fences to see you. Those are the sorts of relationships you want anyway.

Loving someone who doesn't realize how special you are

Ruins how good it should feel to be in a relationship

You're special

It took a day to forget my name

And two days to find another mi amor…

Two days

My well is empty these days

I gave all my water away to the wrong people

They had no interest in restoring what they drank

Take take take

I can go on for so long before

I need water

And everyone is thirsty

Empty well

This hole in my heart can only be filled by me.

Waking up

You won't find anyone like me.

I come around once in a lifetime.

Here

She changes like the seasons.

Be prepared to grow with her.

She grows

You only want me because you can't have me anymore…

You're a good person who deserves good friends. You don't have to deal with selfish, unreliable people who aren't uninterested in you. You can find better than them.

Bruised

But not defeated

We heal quietly in silence

Heartbreak swallowed by madness and storms

Tears, much like rain

The heart wants what it wants

I say

Notetaker

The cameraman shines lights on my face

I documented where contact was made

Recanted my confession

To spare yours

It was a lie

I swore

Unable to identify the knife

I never walked away

My feelings stayed in the same place

You stepped from

To this very Saturday

I was too young and immature to tell you how much you

Meant to me

Everyday

I could have said

Thank you

I could have

Wherever you go

You're still mine

I visit your sleep

I appear in your dreams and memories

I am the warm kiss on your cheek

The small laugh in your throat

Whisper in your hair

I am in everything you see

Missing me

You remember my taste

Grazing your teeth

Worse than a narcotic

A contagion

I am a recurring flu

I'm all you'll ever need

I'm everything you'll ever be

I've tried to call you a thousand times

I never go through with it

Phone calls

Shoot to kill

Aim for the mark

Heartbeat

Fire

Bullseye

Aim

It's hard letting go of the good

Wishing I could take you and me back there

Back in time

There's no convincing them to love you or giving them gifts. It's time to leave. No reason to stay around, hoping they made a mistake. There's no convincing love to love lost.

I fell in love with the sun

On a rainy day

Predictable forecast

Blown away

I find myself

Dancing in soaked shoes

Jacket is nowhere to be seen

Rain poured, flooding my senses

Water came too fast

Lighting and thunder roared from within

I chose you

Rain came expectedly

Unpredictable weather

You gave them everything.

That's why you can't get over them.

My all

When you pulled away, you took my heart with you…

Come back

It's brutal learning how to walk without you.

I'm adjusting to listening to my footsteps.

Lonely ride

You'll be happy to know that I'm not a pushover
anymore…

Pushover

I should have kissed you a little longer

Held you to my chest a second more

Told you more about me

Opened up so you could see the rest of me

Been more honest about how you made me feel

I should have been more selfish

You were mine to steal

I should have told you no when it mattered

I should have made you come when you said no

I should have put my foot down and held my own

Should have fought

Sometimes ran

I should have listened to you more

Trusted your intentions

I shouldn't have called you so many times

I should have let you see me cry

I should have

How do you fall asleep without me wishing you a good night?

Goodnight

Your enough won't always be enough for everyone. You can be the greatest you in a relationship and pull out all the stops, but if they're not feeling it, they'll find a reason to leave. They have the right to go when they please. Remember, you are enough, maybe not for them, but for someone looking for what you're selling.

For sale

I haunt your mind

Because you're still mine

The undead

In the beginning, you said you would leave me

And

I thought giving you my heart would make a
difference.

Careful listener

I fought and fought

But the battle was lost

I lay wounded on the battle floor

For months

Reenacting the carnage in my head

Surrender

I was impossible to love

I made it impossible for you

A broken heart

I was too embarrassed to let you see

It wasn't big

Rather small and fragile

My fears

Kept shoving you back

From holding a damaged little thing

No one close to me had ever seen

Tiny hearts

It's possible to meet your soul mate in the wrong season. You two might have everything in common, but their life is too chaotic to build a stable foundation. You want it to work, but you're both too immature to create a relationship healthy enough to thrive.

Too early

Sorry to call

I thought it was last year

My heart dialed your number

I can say this time without tears

Sorry to bother

Sorry to reminisce

It's the what-ifs

That is the hardest to kill

You have to go

I know

I thought I'd call

To tell you sorry

For missed phone calls

Sorry to call

On your day off

Accidental calls

I stayed after the party was over

Thinking

You would return

To retrieve what you left

On the dance floor

The lights turned off

The music finally stopped

The guests had their fun

I refused to dance with anyone

Who wasn't you

Music stopped

Nights without you go on forever…

Long nights

You were in too much pain to love

But here I was

Yours

It's aggravating giving when your cup is dry

And she craves something to drink

She craves it more than air

She's so desperate to feel something

Anything of value from you

She would celebrate a drop

And imagine it streaming into her mouth

So she would have something of yours

To cling to

Just a drop

We didn't have to be strangers…

You did what was best for you

And the absolute worst for me

Selfish thoughts

It hurt like hell when I discovered you never cared...

Truth hurts

To be pulled so close

Then dragged so far

You compare both

Wondering what I did wrong

To be ousted beyond the horizon

Where light does not reach

Here I watch it play before my eyes

Here, I seek solace for my broken trust

Elephant graveyard

I hope you find all the peace and love I couldn't give you…

My wish

I taught you what love looked like, from your hair to your toes. I showed you how love goes. The ins and outs, and how to communicate. I taught you which love language you should worry about. I was your right hand. I taught you how to feel important. Be the prize—the mission. I taught you how to hug. I made you feel the things you were missing. I built you high. I praised you when you felt low. A consistent rock, I kept you warm in the cold. You needed nothing. Whole, you ran back to secondhand love, missed calls, horrible conversations, confusion, and poor commitment.

Stray

Reading old texts will break you all over again…

Delete them

She walks to her doom

But so in love

She can't see the red lights

Flashing in her face

Hazard lights

We don't talk anymore, and that's okay. I'm not bitter or sad or mad or disappointed. You grew apart from me. You needed to stretch your legs and run. I'm still learning how to walk. The conversations you wanted weren't what I wanted to have. You wanted to travel. I had to stay home and build a life for one. You outgrew me. You got used to me. My voice no longer inspired you. My words bored you. I wasn't fun anymore, and you wanted out. A stickler in my ways, a student of the discipline, I had become ridged. You had to fly. I wish you the best. I wish you happiness. I hope you find everything you are looking for. A phone call, maybe dinner with a view—I'll work up the courage to call and say hello. Perhaps you'll call before me.

I look forward to that.

Sometime soon

About the author

Ry Reed has written poetry for many years. Poetry has helped her heal, and she uses her life as a platform to teach and share lessons she's learned along her journey. Depression, heartbreak, and willingness to move forward and start over again, her poems are relatable, personal, and straight to the point. Her every word digs out emotions and encourages change. She lives in southern California with her mother and brothers and writes poetry, non-fiction, and fiction books.

LATE NIGHT DRIVES TO YOU

https://ryreedthewriter.com/

ISBN: 9798865690603

Subjects: Poetry/ Love/ Romance

Summary: This story is not a romance or a fairy tale. These poems are a cautionary tale, a warning to seek the best people to love and to protect your heart against those who wish to break you. They come charming, sweet, romantic, and with luscious promises to adore you. But that's how the tragedy starts. The beautiful damsel was lured to her doom on a warm summer night. Her car was found abandoned, her heart missing.

Click Latest Releases

Pink Grapefruit

Ry Reed

White Orchids

Ry Reed

Walking
on
the
Moon

Ry Reed

A WELL OF THOUGHTS

Ry Reed

Ry Reed's social media

NSTAGRAM: @ry.reed.the.writer

PINTEREST: Ry Reed the writer

YOUTUBE: Ry Reed the Writer

FACEBOOK: ryreedauthorandpoet

WEBSITE: https://ryreedthewriter.com/

You made it to the end!
Now it's time to leave a
review! Share your
thoughts with the world.

Thank you!

Made in the USA
Las Vegas, NV
28 February 2024

86454429R00246